Riddles, Riddles from A to Z

By CARL MEMLING Pictures by TRINA SCHART

GOLDEN PRESS · NEW YORK

Hey diddle, diddle,
A book of riddles,
What can the answers be?
The first starts with A,
The second with B,
And the last answer starts with a Z.
Hey diddle, diddle,
And hey diddle dan!
Answer them all, see if you can.

A

What is it?
It floats like a log.
It looks like a log.
Yet it isn't a log.
It's...
　　An alligator.
A is for Alligator.

B

What is white
when it's dirty
and black
when it's clean?
A blackboard.
B is for Blackboard.

C

What has two hands
but can't scratch itself?
A clock.
C is for Clock.

D What is the hardest key to turn?
A donkey *(don key)*.
D is for Donkey.

E   As I went through a field of wheat,
I picked up something good to eat;
It was white and had no bone,
And in twenty-one days it walked alone.
What did I pick up?
   An egg.
E is for Egg.

F

What is it?
It runs all around the pasture,
yet it never moves.
The fence.
F is for Fence.

G Four fingers and a thumb,
Yet flesh and blood I have none.
What am I?
A glove.
G is for Glove.

H The more you take away,
The bigger I become.
What can I be?
A hole.
H is for Hole.

I

I scream,
You scream,
We all scream —
for what?
Ice cream.
I is for Ice cream.

J

What Jack has a head
but no body?
Jack-o'-Lantern.
J is for Jack-o'-Lantern.

K Acts like a cat,
Looks like a cat,
Yet it isn't a cat.
What is it?
A kitten.
K is for Kitten.

L

What am I?
My fleece is white as snow.
 And everywhere that Mary goes,
I am sure to go.
 A lamb.
L is for Lamb.

M

What is it that makes two people out of one?
A mirror.
M is for Mirror.

N

What always has one eye open?
A needle.
N is for needle.

O

Who is the strange one
who lives in the sea?
He has eight arms but no legs.
The octopus.
O is for Octopus.

P What has a thousand needles
but does not sew?
A porcupine.
P is for Porcupine.

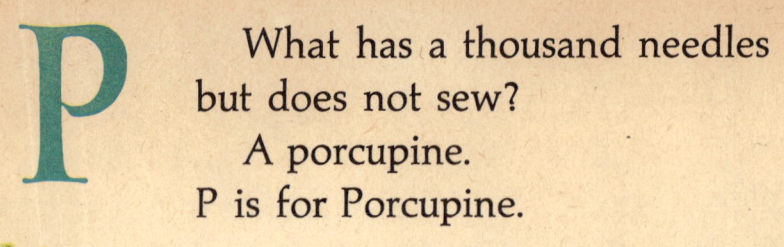

Q

Who is next to a king on his throne?
His queen on her throne.
Q is for Queen.

R What is it that runs in and out of town all day and night? The road. R is for Road.

T

What pets make stirring music? Trumpets *(trum pets)*.
T is for Trumpet.

U

What goes up when rain falls? An umbrella.
U is for Umbrella.